MAKING HISTO

GREECE
in the time of
PERICLES

Written by
Fiona Clarke

Illustrated by
Mark Bergin
John James

SIMON & SCHUSTER
YOUNG BOOKS

Contents

Design	David Salariya
Research	Fiona Macdonald
Editor	Penny Clarke
Consultant	Anton Powell

First published in Italy by
Giunti Gruppo Editoriale, Firenze
under the title Nella Grecia di Pericle

This edition first published in 1993 by
Simon & Schuster Young Books
Campus 400
Maylands Avenue
Hemel Hempstead
Herts HP2 7EZ

Printed in Italy by Giunti Industrie Grafiche

Introduction

THIS BOOK DESCRIBES LIFE in Athens in the time of Pericles who lived from about 495 to 429 BC. For over 20 years Pericles was the most important man in Athens. He was a wise politician and a trusted war leader. He was also a superb orator and his speeches in the Assembly (pages 8 and 9) were eagerly awaited. This is one reason why he remained popular and enjoyed the support of the people of Athens for so long. The other reason was that, despite his rather cold, haughty manner, everyone knew he was absolutely honest.

In Pericles's time, Greece was not a united country as it is today. It was made up of a number of competing city-states, each surrounded by its own territory. While Pericles was in power, Athens was the most important of these city-states and controlled an empire which included much of central Greece and many of the Greek islands. Pericles also set up Greek colonies abroad, in Italy and Turkey.

The wealth and power of Athens made other states jealous, and there were many attacks on the city-state. Pericles showed great skill, both as a politician and as a general, in guiding Athens through difficult and dangerous times.

At the same time Pericles also helped to build one of the most brilliant civilizations the world has known. Architects, artists, potters and sculptors all worked in the city, producing magnificent works of art which are still admired today. Many learned scientists, mathematicians, writers and philosophers made their home in Athens, and contributed to its greatness.

The Athenians had also developed a remarkable system of government called democracy (pages 8 and 9). Instead of one powerful ruler who made all the laws, individual Athenians could take part in governing their city-state. This was the beginning of modern democratic government.

The City-state of Athens

The city-state of Athens was quite small. It was made up of the walled city of Athens and the surrounding countryside. Even the most distant village was only a day's walk from the city centre.

The total population was about 350,000 and more people lived in the countryside than in Athens itself. Rich people – like Pericles's family – had homes in the city and large estates in the country. The people working on these estates were generally slaves. Poorer people who had small farms worked the land themselves. Their children helped with the farm work. The youngest scared birds away to stop them eating the newly planted seeds. Older children herded the sheep and goats that gave their family wool and milk. The oldest boys helped their fathers take the farm produce to sell in the market.

Farmers used oxen to pull carts and ploughs. Mules – a cross between a male donkey and a female horse – were also used for pulling heavy loads, and for other tasks around the farm.

Heavy, bulky goods were transported in large pottery containers.

Some were just big plain jars. Others, called amphoras, were thinner and had two handles to make carrying them easier. Wine was usually transported in amphoras. It was also exported in them. Archaeologists have found the remains of Athenian wine amphoras in many different places, including Italy and North Africa.

▽ Olives were used for food and also made into oil for cooking and lighting. Women and children knocked the ripe olives to the ground with long sticks. Older boys climbed the trees to reach the fruit on the highest branches. The ripe olives were packed in baskets before being crushed in the nearby press. The arm of the press was weighted with stones, but swinging on it increased the pressure! The oil ran from the crushed fruit into big pottery collecting jars. The baskets stopped the olive skins and pits getting into the oil and spoiling it. Olives are still an important crop in modern Greece and Greek olives and olive oil are major exports.

A Centre of Trade

The city of Athens had a large, busy market. Farmers brought their goods to sell: fruit and vegetables, wool, wine and oil. Craftsmen who worked in the city displayed their wares: jewellery, pots, swords and spearheads.

The market attracted traders from all over Greece and from as far away as Italy, Asia Minor (roughly modern Turkey) and North Africa. Many also came to sell. Wheat always fetched a good price. The land around Athens could not grow enough to feed everyone, so supplies from abroad were vital.

▷ Although the market was always crowded, there were far more men there than women. Wealthy women sent slaves to do their shopping; poorer women sent their husbands. The only women on their own were slaves. Those fetching water from the public fountain carried the jars on their heads.

△ The market place was a good place for men to meet their friends, discuss political matters or just catch up with the latest gossip.

The summers in Athens are very hot, so around the central square of the agora, or market place, were shady arcades where the traders set out their goods away from the sun's heat.

Athens is not on the sea, but it has a bustling port: Piraeus. Pericles knew how important the port was for Athens's trade and wealth. He made sure that the state had a strong navy to patrol the sea and to stop pirates attacking ships going to and from Piraeus. Pericles also had walls built to protect the road from the port to the city centre.

△ Occasionally a wealthy woman crossed the market place, going to visit a friend and followed by a slave. If it was hot, the slave held a sunshade over her.

Democracy

The Athenians called their system of government 'democracy', which means 'government by the people'.

How did democracy work? An Assembly was held about every nine days and all citizens could attend. They could suggest topics for discussion, speak in debates and vote on whether to pass new laws. However, only adult males were citizens, so only men could take part in the Assembly.

Athenian citizens also took turns in running the government. Meetings of the Assembly were organized by a committee. Each year the citizens chose the members of the committee. This stopped any one man from becoming too powerful in government.

The committee also chose men to run the government departments for short periods. These departments organized matters like the building of new city walls, or arranging food and weapons for the army. An inner council dealt with day-to-day business.

The army and navy were run in a similar way. The Assembly chose ten war leaders, who served for several years at a time – it could have been disastrous to change generals too often in the middle of a war! Pericles was elected General in 454 BC. The citizens admired him so much they went on re-electing him as General until his death in 429 BC.

1. The Athenians had no clocks or watches. Instead they used water clocks to tell the time.
2. Ceramic (pottery) tablets were used for records of the Assembly's business.

GREECE IN THE 5TH CENTURY BC

A Dinner Party

Wealthy Athenians enjoyed giving dinner parties for their friends. It was a chance to discuss politics, argue about the newest scientific theories or just gossip. But, like democracy, these parties were men-only affairs. The only women present were slaves or musicians.

Even the grandest rooms in a wealthy Athenian's home were furnished very simply. There were couches and low tables and, when it got dark, slaves brought in lamps. While they talked and ate, the diners reclined on the couches set around the room and servants put the food and wine on low tables by the couches.

Greek food was quite plain. Everyday meals consisted of bread, cheese and olives, with whatever fruit and vegetables were in season. Meat and fish were only served on special occasions – such as a dinner party like the one shown here. The main drink was wine, usually with water added. It was drunk from pottery goblets, rather like large wine glasses, or from larger, shallow bowls with two handles to make them easier to hold.

▽ Many Athenians thought the success of a dinner party could be measured by how drunk everyone got! Although there was plenty of drinking they did not smoke because tobacco was unknown. Nor could guests who had drunk too much clear their heads with strong coffee, because that too was unknown, as were tea, chocolate and sugar. Honey was the chief way to sweeten food. Dried raisins were an important part of the winter diet.

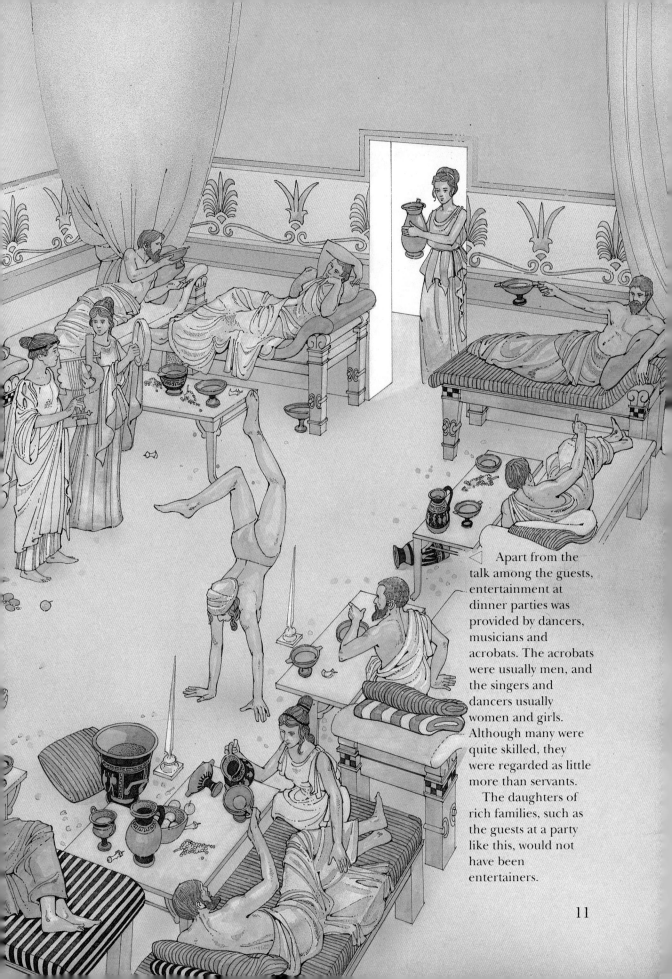

Apart from the talk among the guests, entertainment at dinner parties was provided by dancers, musicians and acrobats. The acrobats were usually men, and the singers and dancers usually women and girls. Although many were quite skilled, they were regarded as little more than servants.

The daughters of rich families, such as the guests at a party like this, would not have been entertainers.

Women at Home

Athenian women lived very different lives to men. Men spent most of their time away from home: attending the Assembly, working in the fields or their workshops, or just meeting and talking to their friends. Women, in contrast, rarely went out; the work they did was based in and around the home.

Athenian households were very self-sufficient. Each family spun and wove the thread to create the cloth from which they made their clothes. They ground their own flour and made their own bread, and preserved fruit and vegetables to eat in winter. This was all done by women.

Girls did not go to school, so their mothers educated them at home. They learnt to spin and weave, to cook and sew, to care for the sick and look after babies and children.

Most Athenian housewives had slaves to help them, so girls had to learn how to give orders to slaves and how to organize the running of a home for when they married.

Women were not allowed to meet or entertain men (except relatives) on their own, but they could go out to visit female friends or relatives. They also went to the theatre – a very popular entertainment. Even so, they would be accompanied by a man – their husband or a slave.

◁ The elaborate hairstyle of the woman busy at her loom suggests that she is the mistress of the house.

▽ Patterns like these, painted or stencilled on the walls, were often the only form of interior decoration in a home.

◁ Elaborate lamps like this one were only found in the homes of wealthy Athenians. The boat-shaped container at the top held oil; when it got dark, a wick resting in the oil was lit. The disc at the back of the lamp reflected the light, so making it brighter.

◁ Archaeologists have found the remains of many toys like these dating from the time of Pericles.

Athens at War

The Greek city-states often fought with each other. Sometimes the wars were little more than quarrels. At other times they threatened the whole country.

The Spartans, a harsh, war-like people based in Sparta, to the south of Athens, were old enemies of the Athenians. The Spartans thought the Athenians wanted to dominate all the other city-states and so gain power over the whole of Greece. The Athenians despised the Spartans and their form of government, which was very different to the Athenians' democracy. The population of Sparta was divided into two main groups. One group consisted of highly trained, upper-class warriors. The other was made up of state-owned slaves, or helots, who worked to support the warriors.

Athenians told a story to illustrate the cold-blooded courage of the Spartans. A young Spartan warrior was preparing to go to war. His mother handed him his shield, saying: 'Come back carrying this shield, or else be carried home on it.' In other words, she would prefer that her son died in battle and was carried home on his shield to be buried, than that he was defeated and his shield taken away by his enemy. This was the fate that awaited all captives and, to the Spartans, it was a terrible disgrace.

Athens and Sparta were at war for most of the time Pericles was an important politician. The Spartans were much better trained and equipped than the Athenians but, thanks to Pericles's skill, the Athenians were never defeated.

The fierce battles, mostly hand-to-hand combat, cost both sides many of their best fighters. Providing food and weapons for the soldiers was also very expensive for both sides. Pericles was wise enough to realize that neither side could win, and that both were being ruined in the process. He didn't mind about Sparta, of course, but he certainly didn't want Athens ruined. Not all the politicians were as wise, and peace was not declared until 429 BC – after Pericles's death.

Any soldier who died fighting bravely in battle was considered a hero by his fellow Athenians. Every year there was a solemn official ceremony at the site of the Battle of Marathon, where the Athenians had defeated the Persians in 490 BC.

15

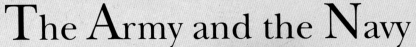

The Army and the Navy

1–2. Shields carried into battle by Athenian soldiers. They were of wood covered with bronze.
3. Painting from a ceramic (pottery) vase showing soldiers ready for battle.
4. An Athenian soldier in full armour, about 480 BC. His helmet is decorated with horsehair, and his breastplate is strips of linen reinforced with metal discs.

5. A trireme dating from about 485 BC. These ships had a crew of some 200: 170 oarsmen, 14 soldiers, 15 sailors and the captain. There was also a piper who set the rhythm and pace for the oarsmen. Sheets of leather protected the top row of oarsmen from the enemy's arrows and javelins. With so many men on board, there was no room for provisions, so each night the triremes had to find a sheltered bay or safe harbour where everyone could land.
6. Cross-section of a trireme.

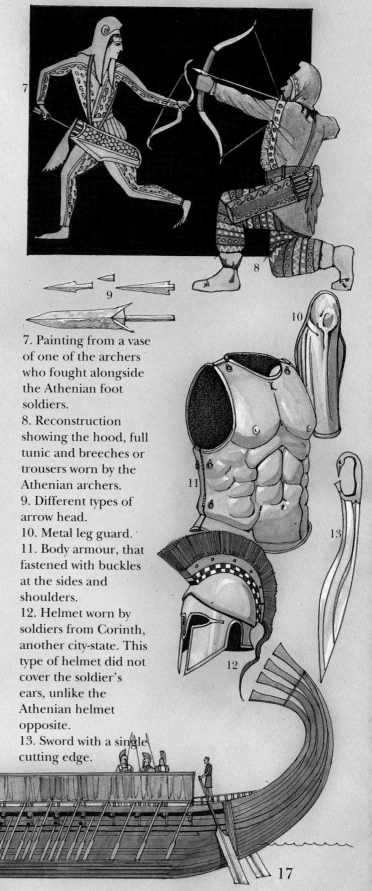

Sparta had a permanent army, Athens did not. Instead, all Athenian men had to be ready to fight in defence of the city whenever it was threatened.

The Athenians fought many wars, but each period of fighting was quite short, because the men had to be home in time for the harvest. If the crops were not harvested, there would not be enough food for everyone to eat that winter. The Spartans knew this and often burnt their enemies' crops, hoping they would starve.

The Athenian army consisted mainly of foot soldiers, called hoplites. They wore metal helmets, tough breastplates and metal leg protectors. They fought with swords and spears and carried big shields for protection.

Athens did not have a navy until after the Persians invaded in 490 BC. This invasion, by an enemy from so far away, made the Athenians realize how important a navy was. Their first warships were slow and clumsy. They had to get close to enemy boats so the soldiers could leap on board and fight hand-to-hand, just like a land battle. Later, they used faster boats called triremes.

7. Painting from a vase of one of the archers who fought alongside the Athenian foot soldiers.
8. Reconstruction showing the hood, full tunic and breeches or trousers worn by the Athenian archers.
9. Different types of arrow head.
10. Metal leg guard.
11. Body armour, that fastened with buckles at the sides and shoulders.
12. Helmet worn by soldiers from Corinth, another city-state. This type of helmet did not cover the soldier's ears, unlike the Athenian helmet opposite.
13. Sword with a single cutting edge.

War at Sea

The Persians were the Athenians' most dangerous enemy. Their forces were well equipped and fought very fiercely, both on land and at sea. The Persian invasion of 490 BC was defeated, although the Athenians lost many of their finest warriors in the battle. However, the peace did not last long. The Persians attacked again in 480 BC, breaking through Athens's strong defences.

After the defeat of the Persians in 490 BC, the Athenian Assembly decided that the state needed a navy in order to protect it from more invasions. It was ready just in time to face the second Persian invasion in 480 BC. The navy had been paid for by the chance discovery of a particularly rich vein of silver in the mines at Laurium, where most of the Athenians' silver came from.

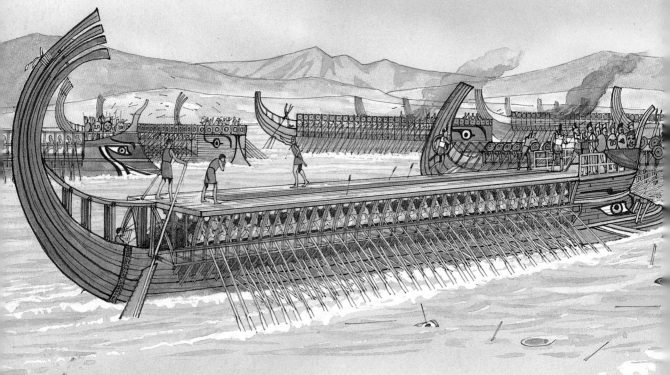

△ The bows (front ends) of triremes were usually painted to make them look very awe-inspiring. Even if all the soldiers on board a boat were killed, the underwater ram meant that the trireme was still a dangerous weapon.

△ A brazier with a fire was always kept on board. This was not to provide warmth, but so that burning torches could be hurled on to the enemy's ships to set them on fire and start a panic among the crew and oarsmen as they tried to escape.

Powered by 170 oarsmen and steered by a man with two long paddles at the stern (back) of the ship, the Athenians' triremes were the best warships of their time. Above the top row of oarsmen was the flat wooden deck. This allowed the soldiers and archers to move around to find the best place to attack the enemy's ships.

The trireme's most effective weapon was the ram. The bow (front) of the boat projected underwater into a kind of beak. If an enemy warship crossed the path of a trireme, the oarsmen increased their rowing rate to ramming speed, so driving the ram into the other boat. This holed the boat below the water level, making it sink.

The Theatre

The Athenians knew how to enjoy themselves. They had many different entertainments to choose from: chariot races, sports, processions and festivals, but the most popular of all was the theatre. Crowds flocked to see the latest plays. Everyone could go, even people who could not afford to pay for their seats, because there were free seats for the poor. There was a wide variety of plays to enjoy: tragedies, historical dramas and comedies.

▽ The theatre was very important to the Athenians and each year they held great drama festivals. Performances went on all day and the audience voted for the plays and the actors they liked best. The winners received prizes and great fame.

One of the most famous of all Athenian dramatists was Sophocles (496–406 BC). He is believed to have written 123 plays, some of which are still performed. He won many prizes at the drama festivals: 96 of his plays won first prizes!

The theatres were in the open air. Summers in Greece are hot and although the winters are cold, they are quite short, so that sitting outside to watch a play was usually very pleasant.

The auditorium, the part of the theatre where the audience sits, was built in a large semi-circle around the stage area. The audience sat on stone terraces, not on separate seats. The theatres were very cleverly built, so that people sitting in the row furthest from the stage could see and hear everything that was going on as well as those sitting near the stage.

Because the theatres were in the open air, stage lighting was unnecessary and there was no scenery as we know it today. Most of the plays were based on well-known stories, which the audience already knew.

In Greek theatre, all the parts were played by men and there were no actresses. Some 2,000 years later in England, when Shakespeare wrote his plays, the female roles were also performed by men or boys. Some of the plays the Athenians watched have survived and are still performed today. A few of the comedies are very rude!

Sports

The most famous sporting event in the world, the Olympic Games, was started in Greece, probably in 776 BC. Many of the sports popular then still feature in the Olympics: running, jumping and throwing the discus or the javelin.

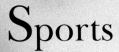

Athenian men were very keen on sport. The city had many gymnasiums where men could go to practise their favourite sport, take a little exercise, or just chat to friends and watch other men take exercise. Women, of course, were not allowed to take part in any sport; their place was in the home.

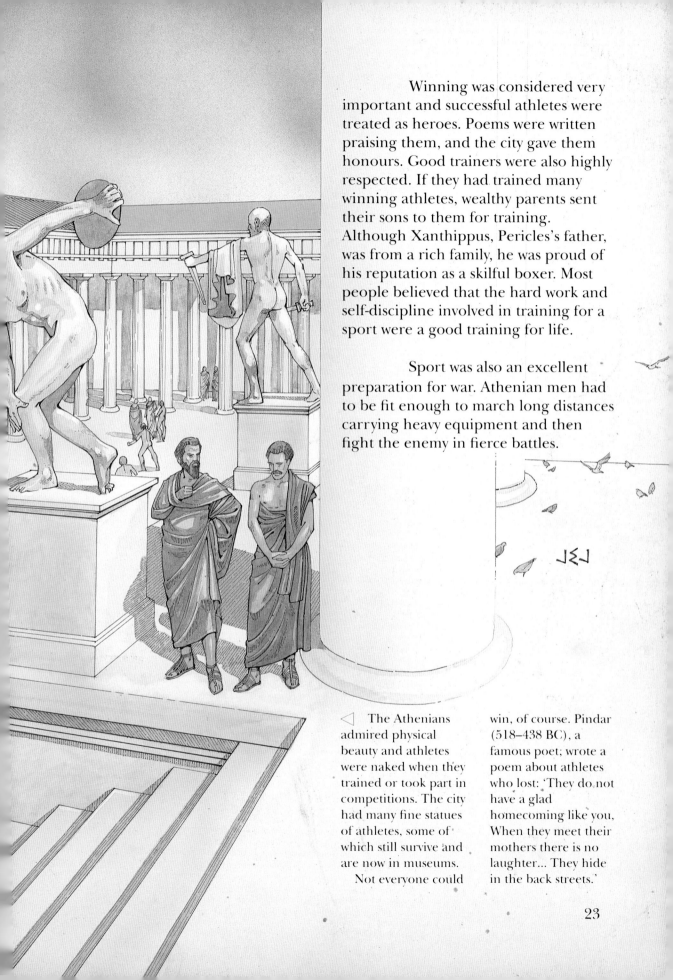

Winning was considered very important and successful athletes were treated as heroes. Poems were written praising them, and the city gave them honours. Good trainers were also highly respected. If they had trained many winning athletes, wealthy parents sent their sons to them for training. Although Xanthippus, Pericles's father, was from a rich family, he was proud of his reputation as a skilful boxer. Most people believed that the hard work and self-discipline involved in training for a sport were a good training for life.

Sport was also an excellent preparation for war. Athenian men had to be fit enough to march long distances carrying heavy equipment and then fight the enemy in fierce battles.

◁ The Athenians admired physical beauty and athletes were naked when they trained or took part in competitions. The city had many fine statues of athletes, some of which still survive and are now in museums.

Not everyone could win, of course. Pindar (518–438 BC), a famous poet, wrote a poem about athletes who lost: 'They do not have a glad homecoming like you, When they meet their mothers there is no laughter... They hide in the back streets.'

Building the Parthenon

When the Persians attacked Athens in 480 BC they destroyed much of the city. After they were defeated Athens had to be rebuilt. The Assembly, encouraged by Pericles, decided that the new temples and public buildings should be even more magnificent than before. The most important of these buildings was a shrine to Athene, the city's own goddess. She was a warrior and the Athenians believed she had helped them defeat the Persians.

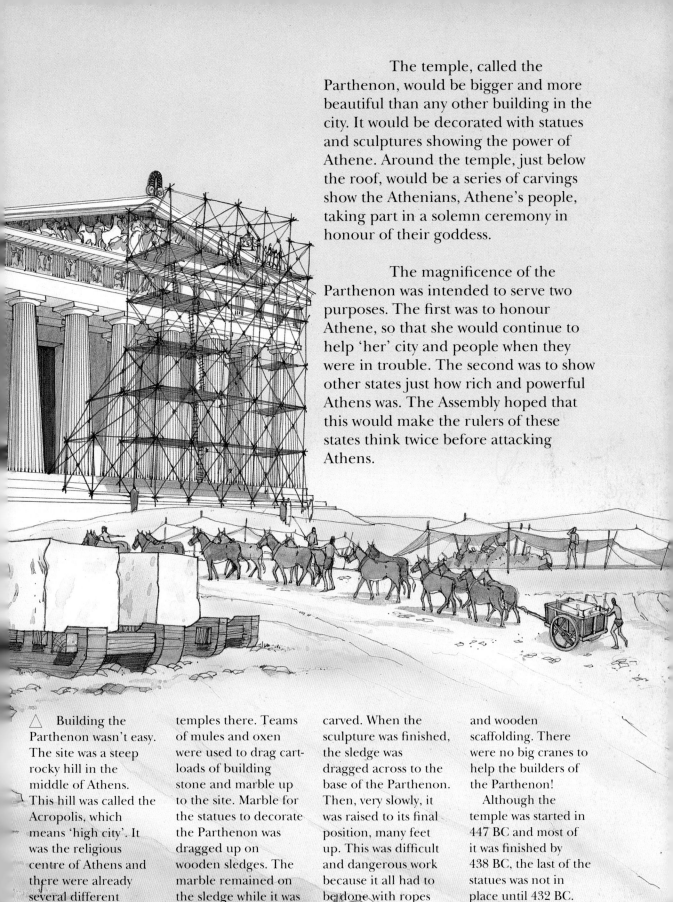

The temple, called the Parthenon, would be bigger and more beautiful than any other building in the city. It would be decorated with statues and sculptures showing the power of Athene. Around the temple, just below the roof, would be a series of carvings show the Athenians, Athene's people, taking part in a solemn ceremony in honour of their goddess.

The magnificence of the Parthenon was intended to serve two purposes. The first was to honour Athene, so that she would continue to help 'her' city and people when they were in trouble. The second was to show other states just how rich and powerful Athens was. The Assembly hoped that this would make the rulers of these states think twice before attacking Athens.

△ Building the Parthenon wasn't easy. The site was a steep rocky hill in the middle of Athens. This hill was called the Acropolis, which means 'high city'. It was the religious centre of Athens and there were already several different temples there. Teams of mules and oxen were used to drag cart-loads of building stone and marble up to the site. Marble for the statues to decorate the Parthenon was dragged up on wooden sledges. The marble remained on the sledge while it was carved. When the sculpture was finished, the sledge was dragged across to the base of the Parthenon. Then, very slowly, it was raised to its final position, many feet up. This was difficult and dangerous work because it all had to be done with ropes and wooden scaffolding. There were no big cranes to help the builders of the Parthenon!

Although the temple was started in 447 BC and most of it was finished by 438 BC, the last of the statues was not in place until 432 BC.

The Parthenon

Pericles asked Iktinos, a famous architect, to design and oversee the building of the Parthenon. Work began in 447 BC. The Acropolis had been a religious site for many years, so Iktinos had to get his workmen, mostly slaves and prisoners-of-war, to clear away the remains of earlier buildings before work could begin.

The temple was built of sparkling white marble, cut from quarries at Mount Pentelicus, a few miles north-east of the city. Rows of tall columns surrounded the central chambers where the religious ceremonies took place. Today, even though the Parthenon is a ruin, it is still admired as one of the most beautiful buildings in the world.

While Iktinos was supervising the construction of the temple, another famous artist, Phidias, supervised the decoration. Phidias was a friend of Pericles and a well-known sculptor. He directed the teams of craftsmen who did the actual carving. Many of the sculptures were more than life-size – they had to be because otherwise no-one on the ground would have been able to see them once they were in position high up just below the roof of the Parthenon.

1. The columns of the Parthenon are in a style called Doric.

2. Originally, some of the decorations were in colour.
3. Reconstruction of decoration on the north of the temple, showing part of the procession in honour of Athene (see page 30).

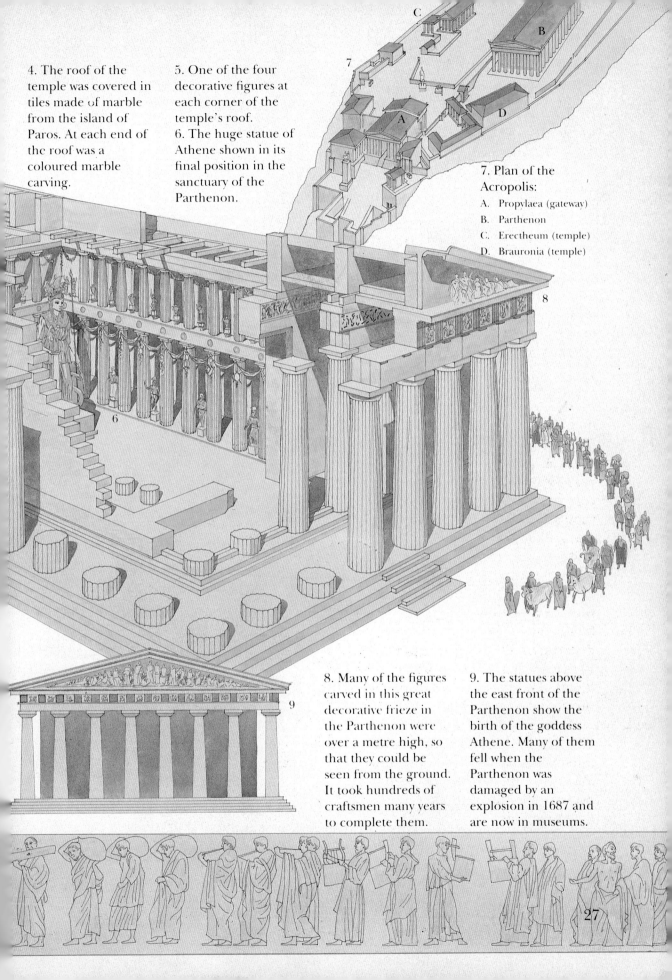

4. The roof of the temple was covered in tiles made of marble from the island of Paros. At each end of the roof was a coloured marble carving.

5. One of the four decorative figures at each corner of the temple's roof.

6. The huge statue of Athene shown in its final position in the sanctuary of the Parthenon.

7. Plan of the Acropolis:

A. Propylaea (gateway)
B. Parthenon
C. Erectheum (temple)
D. Brauronia (temple)

8. Many of the figures carved in this great decorative frieze in the Parthenon were over a metre high, so that they could be seen from the ground. It took hundreds of craftsmen many years to complete them.

9. The statues above the east front of the Parthenon show the birth of the goddess Athene. Many of them fell when the Parthenon was damaged by an explosion in 1687 and are now in museums.

The Statue of Athene

The Greeks worshipped many different gods and goddesses. Like other early peoples, the first Greeks had been frightened by things they did not understand, such as thunder and earthquakes. To try to tame these natural forces, the Greeks made them into gods, gave them names and worshipped them. They hoped that the gods would be pleased and so leave them in peace. Zeus was the god of thunder and Poseidon the god of earthquakes. Other gods and goddesses became the guardians of a particular city or people.

The warrior Athene was Athens's own special goddess. The statue of her that Phidias designed was enormous. It completely dominated the inside of the Parthenon. Although destroyed many centuries ago, archaeologists believe that it was over 10 metres tall, so making ordinary humans feel very small in the goddess's presence. Made of wood covered with gold and ivory, the statue gleamed by day and at night glowed mysteriously in the temple's dim light.

Athene was dressed as a warrior with a figure of victory in one hand. Her other hand rested on a massive gold shield. This shield caused trouble. Phidias decorated it with figures of gods – and himself and Pericles! The Assembly was outraged at this insult to their goddess and Phidias was banished from Athens.

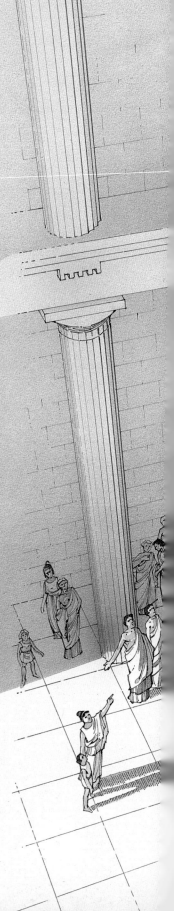

▷ The statue of Athene was ready to put in the Parthenon in 438 BC. Getting it in place was not easy. It was long and heavy, but the Athenian builders were very skilful. Tall, strong scaffolding was built to support the statue as it was gradually levered upright and into position.

A special column was put up to support the figure of winged victory in the goddess's outstretched hand. This statue, too, was made of wood covered with gold and ivory.

Once the scaffolding was taken down and the Parthenon had been dedicated to Athene, ordinary people were not allowed inside to point and stare at the magnificent statue of their city's goddess.

Athene's Festival

In 438 BC, the Parthenon was finished and the statue of Athene placed in position. It was time to celebrate. From miles around, crowds flocked into Athens from the countryside to watch the procession and take part in the many colourful celebrations.

A huge procession formed in the market place, headed by horse-drawn chariots. Then followed members of the Assembly, together with Pericles who had been the driving force behind the building of the Parthenon. There were priests and musicians and men leading animals for sacrifice to Athene, just like the sculptures on the Parthenon (see page 26).

As the procession wound its way through the city's streets, it was followed by crowds of ordinary people, dressed in their best, coming to take part in honouring their city's goddess. When the procession reached the great square outside the Parthenon, only the priests and some important citizens were allowed inside.

The festive procession was the first of many. Every four years the people of Athens held a similar festival to honour Athene. A new robe for the goddess was carried at the head of the procession. It was made of goatskin decorated with the face of a monster on the back and around the edge hung tassels that looked like snakes.

MB

Athenians were proud of their rich, powerful city and the magnificent buildings which had risen after the devastation caused by the Persians. Only a state that was both wealthy and confident of its power could afford to spend so much time and labour on such projects. Other states recognized this and were jealous of Athens. They also feared that Athens would dominate the smaller, poorer states.

Even some of Athens's own citizens grumbled at the expense of all the rebuilding, fearing that such a show of wealth would make other states attack. And not everyone was convinced that Athene would come to their rescue – or even that Athene existed!

There was jealousy in the city, too. Some people thought Pericles far too powerful. But Athene's festival was still a good holiday!

Important Dates

All these dates are what historians called 'BC', which stands for 'Before Christ'.

776 First Olympic Games held.
496 Birth of the dramatist Sophocles.
495 Birth of the Athenian statesman Pericles.
490 Greece invaded by the Persians.
 Persians defeated at the battle of Marathon.
480 Second Persian invasion of Greece.
 The Persians break through the walls of Athens.
454 Pericles elected General.

447 Work begins on building the Parthenon.
438 Death of Pindar.
 Most work on the Parthenon completed.
 The great statue of Athene put in place in the Parthenon.
 The Parthenon dedicated to Athene.
432 Work on the last of the Parthenon's statues finished.
429 Death of Pericles.

Index